No matter how good your tax professional is, if you don't provide all of the necessary information and figures, your tax return will be wrong.

DO MY BUSINESS TAXES PLEASE

A Financial Organizer for Self-Employed

Individuals & Their Tax Preparers

By

KiKi Canniff

DO MY BUSINESS TAXES PLEASE

A Financial Organizer for Self-Employed

Individuals & Their Tax Preparers

TAX YEAR _____

Legal Disclaimer

The information in this book was published for the purpose of providing tax education to U.S. taxpayers and small business owners, and not for providing accounting or legal advice. The author does not make express or implied warranties in regard to the use of the enclosed information.

Cover Design

Heather Kibbey - Northwest Publishers Consortium - Lake Oswego, OR - www.NPCBooks.com

Publisher

One More Press – www.OneMorePress.com

ISBN #978-0941361-37-8

TABLE OF CONTENTS

DO MY BUSINESS TAXES PLEASE

A Financial Organizer for Self-Employed

Individuals & Their Tax Preparers

HOW THIS ORGANIZER WORKS

This Financial Organizer is for men and women who are in business for themselves. For some of you it's your first tax season as a sole-proprietor or self-employed person; others have been working for themselves for years.

This book can be used as an annual all-at-once organizer to get a year's worth of income and expenses ready for your tax preparer, or you can use it to handle your business records monthly, quarterly, or anytime the bank asks for a financial report.

This organizer will teach you a quick and easy system for getting on top of your business income and expense receipts, and in a manner that will satisfy the IRS.

Maintain this organizer monthly and you will be done in 20-30 minutes each time. The grand prize is realized when tax time rolls around; with this system it takes less than an hour to get ready for your tax professional.

This organizer is especially useful if you are working in an industry that the IRS has classified as a hobby activity. Tracking the income and expenses for a hobby activity is the same as for a small business; both must be done according to IRS rules if you expect to survive a tax audit.

This recordkeeping system does not require a computer, and you need no special math or bookkeeping skills to make it work. After a month or two you may find that it takes only a few minutes a month to keep your business finances in order. All of the forms necessary for making this organizer work are contained in this book.

What You Need

Basic math is the only skill you need to use this financial organizer.

You will also need the following:

- All of the forms found in this book
- 26 large envelopes
- Adding machine

Fill out the forms in this book and your tax professional will have everything necessary to prepare your U.S. small business income tax return.

These forms will help you to manage home office expenses, track cash and tip income, handle inventory according to IRS rules, get the most out of your mileage and trip expenses, get full credit for employee and/or independent contractor costs, and help you to survive a tax audit.

The envelopes can be 6x9 if you don't have many receipts or bigger if your business generates lots of paperwork.

If you buy an adding machine with a paper tape you'll make fewer mistakes. Running a paper tape twice is a terrific way to check your math; when the numbers don't match you've entered something wrong. Add them again until you get two matching numbers.

The organizational process is fairly simple, once you've learned the rules. And, this book includes lots of tips for making the whole process faster next year.

OPERATING AS A BUSINESS

The IRS classifies some business categories as hobby income. If your business falls into one of these categories you will need to do a little extra paperwork to make your business audit proof.

Possible hobby activities, according to the IRS, include taxpayers working in any of the following professions or activities, especially those who work part time.

Airplane or Yacht Charters & Rentals

Artists & Photographers

Auto or Moto-cross Racing

Bowling

Craft or Direct Sales

Dog Breeding or Showing

Entertainers

Farming or Fishing

Gambling

Horse Racing or Breeding

Stamp Collecting

Writing

What all hobby activities on the IRS list have in common is their recreational aspect. Plenty of working people relax by taking pictures, showing dogs, gambling or stamp collecting. When hobby activities produce income it is reported as miscellaneous income and only those hobby expenses that do not exceed the hobby income are deductible.

Hobby activities are not profit motivated, and according to IRS rules in order to report your income and expenses as a business, you must be engaged in making "actual and honest" efforts to produce a profit. The desire for a little extra spending money is not enough to prove to the IRS that you are operating a business.

If you are a hobby dog breeder, for example, which according to the IRS is someone who breeds and/or shows dogs to promote the breed or win favor, you are not in business. The pet owner who occasionally has a litter of puppies is not operating a business. However, they are still required to declare all income from that litter.

Example: *Marty and his sister Sharma each bought a collie pup in 2007. Sharma's dog is a male from one kennel; Marty's is a female purchased from another breeder. In 2010 Marty and his sister bred the two dogs and sold seven puppies for $800 each. Total income $5600.*

They have not as yet decided if there will be future litters. Deductible expenses for the adult dogs are minimal, because they are pets. In fact, because there is no stud fee Sharma's male has no deductible expenses at all, unless the breeding results in the need for veterinary care.

Breeding the dogs is clearly not a business activity; it is a rare event. Even if they intend to make money with this litter, they are not establishing a business. That is what makes it a hobby. The cost of the two adult dogs is not deductible. They are pets.

Deductible expenses for the pregnant female begin with the breeding and end with the weaning, unless there are medical expenses. Since all of the puppies were sold, 100% of her food and medical costs are deductible against puppy sale income. If one of the seven puppies had been kept as a pet by Marty, 1/7 of those expenses would not be deductible because they are for a personal pet. With one less sold, the income would also be lower.

If food and medical attention during the pregnancy cost $1200, $600 was spent on whelping supplies, and another $1200 was spent on food, medical and registration expenses for the puppies, the total expenses for the litter would be $3,000. Marty's profit is $2600; if he and his sister are splitting the profit they would each post $1300 worth of miscellaneous income to their tax return.

If medical complications had resulted in an additional $3,000 worth of veterinary expenses, bringing Marty's total costs to $6,000, his losses would be limited to $5,600, the total income received. If he and his sister were splitting the income and expenses they would each report miscellaneous income of $2800 and miscellaneous expenses of $2800.

The fact that a taxpayer gets personal pleasure out of an activity is not sufficient reason for that activity to be classified as a hobby, as long as that person can prove that they are engaged in the activity for the purpose of making money.

Losing money during the start-up stage of a new business activity does not necessarily indicate that this activity is not engaged in for profit. But, if those losses continue beyond the customary start-up period, or are due to bad business risks or reverses, it could indicate that a particular activity is not profit motivated.

However, if those losses are sustained because of circumstances beyond the control of the taxpayer, including depressed market conditions, such losses would not be an indication that an activity is not engaged in for profit.

A series of prior tax years during which a net profit was posted would be strong evidence that your activity is for profit, even in years when the business lost money.

Regular bookkeeping is one factor that the IRS can use to separates business income from hobby income. A business tracks income and expenses often, so that they can make financial adjustments quickly. Hobbyists are not concerned with the lack of profits. The forms in this book allow you to track your expenses monthly.

If you work in one of the "hobby" industries, proving that you are profit-motivated allows you to deduct all normal and necessary business expenses, even if those expenses exceed your business income.

In an audit technique guide developed for IRS compliance officers, auditors are taught that red flags on a "hobbyist's" tax return include:

- Large, unusual or questionable deductions
- Missing tax schedules
- Inconsistencies on tax returns from various years

And, you can bet they're also watching for:

- Travel expenses that exceed profit potential
- An RV purchased for travelling to and from events
- Part time operations
- Income or expenses that don't meet the industry standards

When determining whether or not an activity is operated as a hobby or as a business the IRS considers the following questions. The more yes answers you have, the better your chances are for beating the hobby classification.

1. Does the time and effort put into this business indicate an intention to make a profit?

2. Does the taxpayer depend on the income from this activity?

3. If there are losses, are they due to circumstances beyond the control of the taxpayer rather than expenses from the start-up phase of this business?

4. Has the taxpayer changed their methods of operation to improve profitability?

5. Does the taxpayer have the knowledge needed to be successful in this activity?

6. Did the taxpayer make a profit in a similar activity in the past?

7. Does the taxpayer make a profit in some years?

8. Does the taxpayer have a reasonable expectation of profits in the future from the appreciation of assets used in this activity?

Because someone in a potential hobby business is already fighting that hobby classification, it is wise to have your taxes done by a professional, rather than doing them yourself. A good tax professional can answer questions based on your individual tax circumstances; the information in this book only addresses general situations.

Documenting a "Hobby" Business

If you don't operate like a business it will be difficult to prove that your activities are not a hobby, especially if you work part time. But this classification can be beaten; it just means you have to document your business activities.

Begin by getting all licenses and permits necessary to run a business in your city and state. This might include a city business license, county license, USDA or other government agency licenses, and state permits or industry licensing. Figuring out what is required by the government shows the IRS that you are operating like a business.

Liability insurance is another indication that you consider yourself a serious business person. So is business networking.

If you are just getting started, prepare an "In Case of Audit" folder. Put evidence documenting other people making a large profit doing what you do, industry income potential and other items that show the profit you are after into this folder. In case of an audit give this folder to your tax professional; he or she can use it to help prove that you are profit motivated.

If you are building a reputation within local or national groups or trade organizations add this documentation, as well as any awards won by you, your business or products to this folder. A printout showing your internet website would also show your business savvy.

Even when low on funds, a successful business person finds ways to promote their business, so put proof of all guerilla marketing successes into this folder as well. An active customer list, as well as a list of businesses or clients who are waiting for your product, will also go a long way toward showing your intent. These all belong in your "In Case of Audit" folder.

Documenting your day-to-day activities is another good way to show the IRS that you are business minded; depreciating purchased equipment is too. But none of these will do you any good if you're not also actively seeking income. And, in the case of an audit, proving that you are profit motivated will be up to you and your tax professional.

To document your day-to-day business activities just means keeping a simple log on all production and sales efforts. A profit-motivated business owner always keeps records on every product and sales effort so they will know the outcome of their efforts. This allows them to make quick adjustments.

The final chapter in this organizer has enough forms for documenting 260 day-to-day business activities. If you are audited, let your tax professional know that you have these records as well.

Business classes, those taken on how to operate a business, also show profit motivation. Seminars and classes that help you to be better at your craft or profession are legitimate business expenses, but it's the taking of actual business classes that will show the IRS your intent for profit. Accounting classes, sales and marketing seminars, budget forecasting and other classes on how to make your business more profitable all fall into this classification.

The above items, along with a written business plan, regular monthly accounting, quarterly financial adjustments when needed, and a strong marketing plan are all handy tools for fighting an IRS declaration that your small business is a hobby activity.

If your tax return is selected for an audit, stay home and send your tax professional in your place. Because once the IRS thinks you work for the love of it, rather than being profit motivated, it will take a qualified tax professional to prove them wrong.

Armed with all of the information entered into this organizer, along with your "In Case of Audit" folder showing profit motivation, your tax professional should find proving that you are in business, rather than carrying on a hobby activity, nice and easy.

GETTING DOWN TO BUSINESS

If you want the IRS to believe that you are operating a business, then you had better run your activities like a business. You'll find ten Tax Pro Rules sprinkled throughout this book; they apply to the financial end of your business. Following those rules will help protect you in the event of an audit.

In the back of this book you'll find a log for documenting your day-to-day business activities. It has space for the name of the project or activity, time spent and results; to make this log valid you should document every marketing event or project that you engaged in, and retain all receipts as well.

The front portion of this book will teach you a simple method for keeping business records that will satisfy the IRS, and help you to understand what you can and cannot deduct. Once you know the rules, saving money on taxes will become easier.

The right tax accountant can also show you how to protect that business profit by setting up a retirement plan, taking advantage of self-employed insurance deductions, and making tax-exempt investments, which can lower your tax bill even more.

Let's start by learning what to do with your business income. Tracking income is easy, once you learn that first Tax Pro Rule.

Tax Pro Rule #1

Absolutely all business income,

including all cash & tips,

must be deposited into a separate bank account,

one used only for business funds.

To survive an IRS audit, you need to maintain a separate checking account for your business. Otherwise, the IRS can question every deposit and expense co-mingled with your personal funds, and your tax bill may be higher than necessary.

Many banks offer free checking, and it makes no difference to the IRS whether this account is in your personal or business name. So, if you don't already have one, open a business account today, and follow Tax Pro Rule #1.

Tracking business expenses is just as easy, look at Tax Pro Rule #2.

Tax Pro Rule #2

Every penny spent or charged for your business

needs a paper trail. If a receipt

is not provided, you can make your own,

just include all of the necessary details.

When you use your debit card or write a check you leave a paper trail, but following that trail a year later can be confusing. It's a lot easier to work from actual receipts.

Getting a receipt for every purchase is the best method, but you can make your own when a receipt is not available. When writing your own receipt you will need to note the date, how much you spent, what you purchased, and who got the money. Carry a small bound notepad in the car for little purchases; you can sort and total them at tax time. Keep an envelope there too, for stashing loose receipts.

Follow those first two Tax Pro Rules and you'll cut your tax prep time in half next year.

STEP ONE: TRACKING YOUR INCOME

Each month when you receive your bank statement, all you need to do is enter the total income deposited onto the Income Tracking Sheet; this form can be found on page 23.

If you do this simple one-minute income posting procedure each month, at the end of the year it will only take you 5 minutes to total your annual income. While others are stressing over their tax return, you can celebrate the New Year without worries.

Write the amount listed on your bank statement as Total Monthly Deposits, minus any non-income deposits such as loans you have made to your business, onto your Income Tracking Sheet. At the end of the year, when you total all posted deposits, you will have your total income for the tax year.

Get one of your 26 large envelopes and write BUSINESS INCOME across the top. Then, each month after you write the Total Monthly Deposit onto your Income Tracking Sheet, put those bank statements inside the envelope. Business bank statements should always be stored with your business tax records.

If you do any barter, trading your goods or business services with another for goods or services, that too must be reported as income according to the IRS.

Tax Pro Rule #3

Every business barter exchange requires

a paper trail assigning value to your time,

or the product you traded

for another's time or product.

You are expected to count as income the value of every barter exchange. The value of a barter exchange is what you would have charged if that person had paid you in cash. If you trade goods or inventory during a barter exchange, those costs will be deducted along with other expenses; for now we're only concerned with barter income.

Post the total value of all barter exchanges to the front of the Business Income envelope and label it Barter Income. Each month write the total of all barter income on both your Income Tracking Sheet as well as your Business Income envelope.

If you receive money from some unique angle of your work, you should list this income separately on both your Income Tracking Sheet and the front of the Business Income envelope. An example of unique income might be consulting work done by an individual within their specialty field, when consulting is not a part of their regular income.

Looking for Income

Although the purpose of this book is to get your financial records organized on a monthly basis, some of you may be starting out with up to 12 months worth of income and expenses. So let's begin by talking about how to deal with a multi-month stack.

If those records are unorganized you're not totally out of luck; it will just take a little longer to figure out how much money you made in your business so far this year. Most income can be found by answering two questions.

Income Question #1: Where did you deposit the checks?

If you did not maintain a separate business bank account the first place to look would be your personal bank account. Grab the checkbook register and highlight every deposit that was made with business income. Total up all of those business deposits and enter that figure on the front of the Business Income envelope as well as on the Income Tracking Sheet, noting the bank account where it was deposited. You will need to save those checkbook registers with other business receipts, in case of an audit.

If you deposited business income into more than one personal bank account, repeat the above procedure on each account.

Because you have co-mingled funds, the burden of proof will be on you if an audit is ordered. You will be required to prove that all other deposits in those accounts were not business income.

Paychecks will be easy, but any cash gifts or other unsubstantiated deposits will cause problems, and could be taxed as business income. The bottom line in an audit is, if you can't prove otherwise the auditor can count those deposits as income.

This is one of the biggest reasons why you want to open a business checking account, to keep the IRS out of your personal bank account.

Income Question #2: What did you do with the cash?

Cash income can be tricky, especially if you spent it without first depositing it into your business bank account. If you have to look backward to account for all cash income, a good place to start is with major purchases, both business and personal, made right after you received a cash payment.

Business income is taxed whether you receive it as a check, cash, barter, or in any other form. The government wants their share, and if the IRS comes looking, and you have no records, you could end up paying taxes you don't owe.

The only real protection is to deposit ALL of your business cash income into your business bank account. You can do this daily, weekly, or as needed. The IRS rules state that when you do not account for all cash income in a consistent manner, they can decide how much cash income you made based on industry standards, so be sure to document all cash income thoroughly.

If you get audited, and you did not keep proper records, you're sunk. So make a plan to keep better records in the future, do your best to come up with the right amount this year, and cross your fingers that you're not audited.

Post the total of all income found to the front of your Business Income envelope as well as to the Business Income sheet in this organizer. Put all paperwork into the Business Income envelope.

Computing Gross Business Income

Now all you have to do is add all bank deposits, barter values, fees, and cash income posted to your Income Tracking Sheet together. Post these totals in the columns for the last month of income; if you have added January thru July's income together, you would post this amount in the line for July's income. Record those same figures on the outside of the Business Income envelope and put all paperwork inside.

Each month you will need to add all bank deposits, barter values, unique income, and cash income to your Income Tracking Sheet, and put all corresponding papers into your Business Income envelope, after recording the monthly total on the front of the envelope.

The form on the following page is for tracking your income.

	INCOME TRACKING SHEET		
Month	Total Bank Deposits	Unique Income Included in Bank Deposit	Barter & Other Income
January			
February			
March			
April			
May			
June			
July			
August			
September			
October			
November			
December			
TOTAL			
NOTES:			

STEP TWO: TRACKING YOUR EXPENSES

How fast you're done with this step depends on whether or not you're organized. If it's easy for you to get your hands on your business expense receipts, it won't take long at all.

If you're dealing with a year's worth of old receipts, and they're all shoved into a shoe box, you're actually in luck. All you need to do is sort them, and this book teaches you how to do it quickly.

For the totally unorganized, using this monthly organizer for the first time, now is the time when you're forced to search high and low for any receipt or recollection of money spent on your business. Here are some good places to look.

Start with your checkbook register, credit card records, debit statements and bank accounts; highlight all business expenses found. Now dig thru your car, coat pockets, business supply box or purse, and anywhere else you normally shove papers to see if any receipts have been left there. Look thru your personal receipts and see if any business receipts were misfiled.

If you purchase goods to complete work for clients, you may find receipts mixed in with client records. Look around your office or workspace to jog your memory for equipment purchased during the tax year, and in general, do everything you can to locate receipts and reconstruct expense records.

Legitimate business expenses are generally 100% deductible from business income. But, you must know what you spent in order to take that deduction. Guessing is not allowed; without a paper trail you will fail an IRS audit.

If you want to pay less in taxes, take the time to track down every legitimate expense. The savings could easily be several hundred dollars.

Once you have dealt with the old receipts, and entered them according to the following instructions you will be ready to start monthly financial reporting. And, when you do your accounting monthly it goes much faster.

Organizing Expense Receipts

Sorting expense receipts is simple, once you learn what is deductible. This book includes a simple ABC sorting procedure that helps you sort quickly.

Tax Pro Rule #4

Sorting expense receipts

is as easy as ABC, when you use

the business expense alphabet.

To help you organize your expense receipts quickly, you're going to label the rest of those large envelopes now. If you have a large stack of receipts you can also and use them as guides when you sort your expense receipts.

Each month you write all totals on the front of these envelopes, and tuck all receipts inside. Those totals are also written on your Monthly Expense Reports.

Creating Expense Envelopes

Across the top of each envelope, write one of the alphabetical titles from the list below. Use a dark pen so you can see it quickly; keep it near the top of the envelope so it won't get covered by papers as you sort.

Each envelope represents a deductible classification as defined by the IRS.

A   *Advertising & Promotional Expenses*

B   *Bank, Visa & Other Business Interest Paid*

C   *Cleaning Materials & Business Supplies*

D   *Donations to Nonprofit Organizations*

E   *Educational Seminars & Classes*

F   *Fix-it & Repair Expenses*

G   *Gifts*

H Home Office Expenses

I Insurance

J Job Required Licenses & Dues

K Key Operating Expenses

L Legal & Professional Fees

M Meals & Entertainment

N Newspapers, Magazines & Subscriptions

O Office Supplies

P Percentages, Commissions & Fees Paid to Others

Q Equipment Purchased

R Rent Paid

S Shipping & Postage

T Travel

U Utilities

V Vehicle (Car/Truck) Expenses

W Wages & Contract Labor Expenses

X Taxes Paid

Y Your Exhibit, Tournament or Entry Expenses

Z Inventory

Now that you have all of your expense envelopes labeled, read the following information explaining which expenses belong in each category. When you're finished, you'll be ready to sort those expense receipts.

What is Deductible?

Since hobby income is not considered business income, because the intent is not profit motivated, it will be included on your 1040 personal tax return as miscellaneous income. Hobby expense deductions cannot exceed hobby income; these are deducted on Schedule A of your 1040 tax return.

Business profit is calculated using IRS Form Schedule C, before it is posted to your 1040 tax return. IRS rules permit a business owner to deduct every ordinary and necessary expense incurred during the production of, or attempt to produce, legitimate income.

A small business owner can also deduct the expense involved in operating a home office, business mileage or depreciation on vehicles, and interest on business-only debts, including credit cards and home equity mortgages.

If you purchase self-employed health insurance, or make IRA or other retirement deposits, these costs are posted to your personal 1040 tax return, not your Schedule C business return. Your tax preparer will want to know if you had any of these expenses.

Self-employment taxes are often the sole-proprietor's biggest tax bill. But, since this funds your Social Security and Medicare accounts, this is what is known as a "necessary evil". They pay off in the long run, if you're here to collect. These expenses are also posted directly to your 1040 tax return.

The more you know about what you're allowed to deduct, the quicker the sorting process will go, and the more items you will deduct with confidence. Remember, for every legitimate expense you subtract you decrease taxable income, keeping more money in your pocket.

Read the following pages explaining the ABC expense category descriptions before you start to sort.

A - Advertising & Promotional Expenses

This category includes all business cards, phone book ads, newspaper & magazine advertisements, flyer inserts, show sponsorships, ads in exhibit catalogs, coupon books, refrigerator magnets and any other money spent to promote or advertise your business. If you spent money, or traded goods or an employee's services to get your business name or product out to the public, it's deductible.

Tournament and entry fees do not belong in this category. Category Y has been reserved for your exhibit and tournament fees, entry expenses and other contest costs.

B - Bank, Visa & Other Business Interest Paid

Monthly business checking account fees, bank overdraft penalties, business credit card finance charges, annual business credit card fees and business debt interest all belong in this category.

Check all bank, credit card and loan statements for charges; this is a deduction that is often overlooed. If you take out a home equity loan to fund your business, all costs involved in getting the loan, as well as all interest charged on that loan, becomes a business deduction.

C - Cleaning Materials & Business Supplies

This category includes all office cleaning supplies, organizing bins, light bulbs, operating supplies, and coffee for clients. And, all business supplies needed to produce income within your profession.

Business supplies include all of the items you need to perform your work; office supplies, overhead (utilities and rent), and business equipment are not included with business supplies. Those expenses are reported in other categories.

D - Donations to Nonprofit Organizations

All small business donations are taken on your personal tax return; they do not go on your Schedule C business return.

However, some business donations may actually be a promotional or advertising expense. If you make a donation for the express purpose of promoting your business it is deducted on your Schedule C under advertising. This might be the case if you are donating items that belong to your business for a benefit auction. Let your tax preparer know if you have any business donations that could be promotional expenses.

Your time is not deductible as a donation; however, if you pay someone and donate their labor that expense is deductible for a business. Products donated are deducted at cost as removed from inventory.

Donations of goods or artwork with a value of $5,000 or more must include a qualified appraisal for each item donated. You only need an appraisal summary, unless the value exceeds $20,000, then you need the complete appraisal. Call your tax preparer before making a large donation if you are confused.

E - Educational Seminars & Classes

Seminars and classes that will help make you better at what you do to produce income, as well as general business classes, are all deductible.

Remember to record all mileage or travel expenses if you have them; those will be reported along with other mileage and travel expenses. If you only have one receipt for everything, simply make copies for other expense categories and highlight the deductions that should be taken there.

Every small business owners should take business and marketing classes from time to time. It will not only teach you more about making a profit, but, in those early years it will also help to establish your profit motive.

F - Fix-it & Repair Expenses

Equipment repairs, the cost involved in fixing a broken office table, and all other repair and fix-it expenses belong in this category. If you pay a computer expert to solve a computer problem, and you do your business recordkeeping on that computer, that's a fix-it expense. When someone comes out to repair the window air conditioner in your home office, that expense is deducted here as well.

G - Gifts

Each year you can deduct up to $25 per client or vendor, when you give gifts to that client or vendor. Make a note on the back of the receipt for the item given, and add the receiver's name.

Cookies and candy put out for all customers who visit your place of business are not gifts; those are business supplies and belong in category "C".

Meals you take part in do not count as gifts either, they are deducted as meals. If you give a client a restaurant gift card, that would be deducted as a gift. Items taken from your inventory are not expensed as gifts either, those are deducted from inventory on a cost per item basis.

H – Home Office Expenses

If you use one room or more in your home exclusively for business, you may be able to deduct a portion of your home operating expenses. This includes rent or interest and property taxes paid, plus household insurance, all shared utilities, lawn maintenance and cleaning.

How much you get to deduct for shared expenses is based on the size of your home versus the space devoted exclusively to the business. Annual totals for each home office expense needs to be written on the front of the Home Office Expense envelope after you sort; the IRS requires that all home office expenses be listed separately.

Any item used 100% by the business can generally be 100% expensed.

If you own your own home, you should discuss the disadvantages of depreciating your home office with your tax professional before taking this portion of the home office deduction. Depreciation will affect taxes due when you sell your home; you will not be able to exclude the office portion of your personal residence from taxes.

You do not have to depreciate your home to take the other home office deduction.

If you build a shop or office on your property you should discuss this with your tax professional <u>before</u> you begin construction.

I - Insurance

Business and liability insurance are expensed in this category; health insurance is not. If you have self-employed health insurance costs they will be reported on the front of your 1040 personal return, not on your business tax return. Tell your tax preparer if you have self-employed health insurance expenses.

J - Job Required Licenses & Dues

Business and license fees, union dues, and membership fees paid to professional and/or business networking organization are all included in category "J".

K – Key Operating Expenses

Some small business operations have specific key operating expenses. For an automotive repair person this might be the expense of operating their shop; for someone who boards cats it would be the cost of operating the cattery and taking care of the visiting felines.

Key operating expenses do not include rent or utilities, but they would include all business supplies used in the operation of the workspace. Although these expenses could also be classified as Business Supplies, listing them separately will help you to prove that you are running a business, and not engaged in a hobby activity, in years where profits are slim or non-existent.

L - Legal & Professional Fees

All bookkeeping, payroll service fees and legal fees incurred by your business are deductible. Any self-employed person who pays an attorney to look over a contract or prepare legal papers has expenses to deduct here.

Hiring a bookkeeping service to handle paperwork or payroll is also included in this category. Payment for tax preparation will be included here, but only the portion that applies to your business tax return.

Some industries have their own professional fees. A builder might regularly use the services of a surveyor or appraiser; list those fees here. If you are in the business of raising show dogs and you hire a professional handler to show those dogs, that too would be considered a professional fee.

Consulting fees, especially large ones, belong in this category.

M - Meals & Entertainment

If you take clients or business associates out to improve your business relationship, it may be deductible. You must always note the client or associate's name on the back of the receipt, as well as what business you discussed. Business meals are only 50% deductible.

Meals eaten during overnight travel need to be totaled separately. For the larger business the IRS per diem rates are often a better way to expense travel meals; the per diem method requires less work but can only be applied to overnight travel meals. Sole-proprietors must use exact receipts until their business qualifies for per diem calculations.

Entertainment expenses included in this category are those that you attended along with your client. This could be anything from a baseball game to opera, as long as you take that client or vendor for the purpose of improving your business relationship.

If you do not attend, but merely give tickets to a vendor or client, those tickets would be categorized as a gift or promotional expense, and those receipts sorted to "G" if gifts or "A" if promotion. Consider the $25 rule before classifying any entertainment as a gift.

Example #1: Jack buys a block of tickets to the annual home & garden show, and gives them to people who want to have their yards landscaped. He does this because he wants them to hire him to do all of the landscape work.

Jack is trying to get work, and that makes those tickets a promotional expense, not an entertainment expense.

Example #2: Judy is a wedding planner. She agreed to work on a celebrity wedding 300 miles away from home in 2010. She kept her apartment while she was gone, and stayed in a hotel while working on wedding plans.

Her travel and motel expenses will end up in the Travel envelope, but all meal receipts for those 10 nights that Judy spent at the wedding location need to be lumped together in the meal category, with a notation about the length of time spent away from home on this out of town job.

N - Newspapers, Magazines & Subscriptions

Magazines, newspapers and newsletters that you purchase to enhance your business knowledge belong in this category. They do not have to be printed; online subscriptions count as well.

This includes magazines you read to stay current on industry trends, upcoming events or other aspects of your specific business.

For example, the salon owner could deduct hair or nail magazines for both skill improvement and for their clients to read, general magazines left out to entertain waiting customers, and a subscription on business operating procedures.

O - Office Supplies

Office supplies are different from business supplies. Business supplies are specific to your trade or industry; office supplies are used by all small businesses.

Dictionaries and office reference books, paper, photocopies, adding machine tape, computer supplies, paper clips, staples, pens, notepads, appointment books, and other desk or office supplies belong here.

The cost of this organizer can be included in this category since it tames the paperwork.

If you pay another business to send your faxes, that too is an office supply expense.

P –*Percentages, Commissions & Fees Paid to Others*

Some business people have to pay commissions on sales or income. If these commissions are subtracted from your payment before you receive it, they were never included in your income totals. This is generally true with sales commissions, agents' percentages, and consignment fees.

When your income is properly calculated, from deposits made, you are protected from including any prepaid commissions, fees and percentages in your income figures. Only commissions you pay direct are included here.

Q - Equipment Purchased

Any equipment purchased for use in your business, including tools, file cabinets, computers, cameras, calculators, desk lamps, office artwork, professional equipment, etc., must be expensed, or depreciated, over its expected business life.

Tax Pro Rule #5

Any equipment purchased,

with an expected life of two or more years

must be depreciated or expensed

as a Section 179 deduction.

The general rule is, if it will be used for two or more years, and cost over $75, it will need to go here, for a depreciation deduction. In most cases you can deduct the entire expense all at once; using a technique the IRS calls the Section 179 deduction.

Your tax professional will need to know the date of purchase, and cost of each tool or piece of equipment you buy, for your business tax return. Itemize all purchases on the outside of the Equipment Purchased envelope when you sort, including all of the above information required for depreciation.

R - Rent Paid

If you are buying your office building you will include all interest paid on the mortgage in this category. Post this information on the front of the Rent Paid envelope as well.

If you pay rent for an office or workspace, rent tools or equipment, pay for shared space, or have other rent expenses, include all of those costs in this category.

Home office expenses do not belong in this category.

S - Shipping & Postage

Stamps purchased to send out business mail, as well as any UPS, FedEx or other shipping or transport fees paid to send out products or business materials belong in the Shipping & Postage category.

Many independent business people use personal stamps to send out business bills. Buy your own stamps and take the deduction. If you pay shipping to receive an item purchased for inventory, that shipping expense will be included with inventory expenses.

If you receive payments for shipping with orders and deposit the entire payment received, all shipping payments will be reflected in your income. By deducing all shipping expenses you incurred in sending the product to your customer you remove shipping expenses from income.

T - Travel

All business trips and seminar travel expenses, including airfare, tips, taxi or bus, parking, entry fees, and hotel expenses are deductible travel expenses.

Taking your spouse along does not make his or her portion of the trip deductible; only your portion will be deductible unless they too are involved in the business. If a trip includes both business and pleasure days, only a portion of the travel expenses can be deducted.

Overnight business trip meals are also deductible, but need to be listed as a separate total for proper reporting.

If you are away overnight often, write the total number of nights you spent out of town on the front of this envelope, as well as the total spent for overnight travel meals, when you sort.

Put the actual meal receipts with the Meals envelope; clip them together and tag them overnight meal receipts, keeping them separate from other meal receipts.

U - Utilities

If you rent a shop or office space and pay utilities they are deducted here. This includes the electricity, water, internet fees, heat, garbage, office telephone, and cable or music subscription fees used at the office.

All business long distance telephone charges, the cost of a 2nd telephone line at home, or a cell phone that is used exclusively for business, can be deducted here. The cost of your primary household telephone is not deductible, even if you use it for business.

Home office utilities do not belong in this category.

V - Vehicle (Car & Truck) Expenses

If you keep good mileage records you'll pay less tax. That's because for every 100 miles you drive for your business you get to subtract over $50 as an expense.

Tax Pro Rule #6

Unless you have a vehicle

used only for business,

keep a notebook in the car

and write down every single business mile.

Business miles include every trip you make to pick up business or office supplies, drop off business mail, or attend professional classes or seminars. The little trips to drop bills at the post office or run to the office supply store for paper add up quickly, and, with the cost of gas you don't want to miss any business miles you drive. The deduction can be huge, depending on how much you drive.

If you kept a mileage log whenever you ran business errands, simply add up your mileage log and use that total for your deductible business miles. Your total vehicle miles can be approximated, if you have your actual business miles written down.

Write the total miles driven for your business on the front of the Vehicle Expenses envelope.

If you are able to devote one vehicle exclusively to your business, all you need are the odometer numbers at the beginning of year (BOY) and the end of year (EOY). If you took the mileage deduction last year, that EOY mileage figure on last year's tax return will become your BOY figure for this year.

If this is your first year in business, and you didn't write the opening mileage down at the start of your business year, check repair or oil change receipts, they may show your mileage, and figure it out from there.

If more than half of all miles put on a vehicle are business related miles, you should also track actual vehicle expenses to see if this is a better deduction. To take actual vehicle expenses or depreciate your vehicle, you will need to itemize all of the vehicle's expenses on the front of the "V" envelope and save all receipts.

Actual vehicle expenses might include car payments, repair costs, tires or parts purchased, auto insurance, vehicle registration fees, gas, oil, and any other costs involved in operating that vehicle.

If you use more than one vehicle in your business, keep track of miles driven in each vehicle. Note each vehicle's miles separately on the front of this expense envelope.

W- Wages & Contract Labor Expenses

If you have employees, find a quality bookkeeping service; most will handle all of the regulatory paperwork for a small fee. Payroll requires regular deposits of taxes withheld as well as deposits of matching sums. Most small business owners don't have the time to add payroll to their "to do" list; lots of qualified bookkeeping companies offer this service.

At the end of the year they can furnish payroll reports showing where all of the money went that did not go directly to the employee. You will need these numbers when your tax return is prepared; put all payroll reports in the Wages & Contract Labor Expenses envelope, after writing totals on the front.

When you hire independent contractors, who are not incorporated, the IRS requires you to file a 1099M form reporting all earnings paid to each person, if you pay them $600 or more during the tax year. These forms can be purchased at any office supply store and must be put in the mail by January 31st. A copy is also sent to the IRS.

If you get caught avoiding payroll taxes by claiming an employee as an independent contractor, the IRS can fine you heavily, and make you pay all unpaid taxes, even those normally paid by the employee.

Someone who works exclusively for you, on your time schedule, doing a job exactly the way you instruct, using your tools or office space, is probably not an independent contractor. You may have an employee, even if they only work a few hours a week, which means you are required to classify them as an employee and follow all laws regarding payroll.

If you're confused about the difference between an independent contractor and an employee, discuss this with your tax professional. An error here now could be expensive later.

X - Taxes Paid

The letter T was already used and taxes are by law required to be eXact and so "X" was chosen to represent taxes. This is where you enter all state sales taxes, city taxes and any other taxes paid for your business.

Don't forget to record your quarterly federal and/or state income tax installment payments. If you pay property taxes on your business building, they too belong here. If taxes were withheld from any payments you received you will need to list those here as well.

Any license required by the state, county or city to operate a business, or to practice your profession, also gets sorted into this category. Your vehicle license does not belong here. If you are expensing your vehicle the license receipt would go with other vehicle expenses.

Y – Your Exhibit, Tournament or Entry Expenses

If participating in contests, tournaments or shows is part of your business, you should track those expenses separately. For example, if you show dogs you will want to include all dog show expenses in this category. Professional gamblers will track tournament fees here, and photographers will log contest entry fees.

All exhibit or tournament fees, event photography expenses, show setup costs, booth sitting fees and any other costs incurred at the event belong in this category. Event mileage and meals are expensed under Travel and Meals.

Clothing purchased to wear while participating in events is not a tax deductible expense, unless you are an entertainer who requires a costume.

Z - Inventory

Inventory is represented by Z because most independently employed people do not have inventory. If you deal in services, or purchase items only to finish a project for a client, you will not have inventory. Although most of you will not need this category it is useful to understand how inventory works in the eyes of the IRS.

Tax Pro Rule #7

All items purchased or created for resale,

are considered inventory by the IRS.

Inventory expenses can only be deducted

as that inventory is sold.

Inventory expenses are deducted on a cost per item basis, and not deducted completely until every item is sold or removed from inventory. As you sort through receipts, pull every receipt that has anything to do with inventory, including shipping charges, and put them into this category.

If you do not purchase items for resale you will not have inventory. If you sell everything the same year that it is purchased, there is no inventory.

At the end of each tax year you will need to count all remaining inventory both in your office and on consignment with others. Your end of year inventory value and count for this year will become the beginning count and inventory value on next year's tax return.

Sorting Your Expense Receipts

Once you understand the categories, and have your expense envelopes labeled, lay your labeled envelopes out on an empty table or desk. Eliminate any envelopes that you know you will not use. For example, you may not have inventory, home office deductions, or meal expenses; which would take three envelopes off the table.

For a multi-month sort space the remaining envelopes far enough apart to avoid mixing receipts when you sort. The monthly sort will be much simpler, once you have dealt with that big stack of old receipts.

Go through all of those receipts, one by one, and decide where each receipt belongs. Lay the receipt on top of the proper expense envelope. Some receipts could be classified in more than one way; unless this book states otherwise just choose the one you think fits best.

To make the sort go quicker, put anything you cannot immediately classify into a "second run" pile. After sorting all of the easy receipts, go back to that stack and try again. Any that you can't figure out, simply clip together and take with you to your tax appointment; they can be dealt with individually when your taxes are prepared.

If you run inventory, don't forget to put all expenses involved in receiving and producing that inventory on top of the Inventory envelope, even though it may also qualify for another category.

Generally, all business expenses will easily fall into one of these abc expense categories.

In the future you will only be dealing with one month's receipts at a time. Instead of sorting them on a table, you can simply mark each receipt with the proper expense letter, sort and total.

Staple each letter pile together, write the month and total on the top receipt, enter the month and total on the front of the proper expense envelope and the proper Monthly Expense Report, and place all receipts inside that same envelope.

Posting Business Deductions

In Step Three you will post all of those Monthly Expense Report totals onto a two-page form. For now, set the Inventory envelope aside. Inventory expenses are explained separately, as they are handled differently.

If you discover additional receipts later, simply scratch out the old total and write the new total on the envelope and put those receipts inside. You will need to change the total on the Monthly Expenses Report and anywhere else you have posted it as well.

When you're all done with your taxes, you'll store all of these expense envelopes in a bag or box marked Tax Receipts. Rules for saving tax receipts and storage tips are addressed in the final chapter of this book.

Tracking Inventory

Inventory only includes items purchased for resale. If you make a product to sell to others you may have inventory; this includes the purchase of animals for resale in a non-farm operation. Animals added to inventory include the cost of the animal as well as any tests or vaccinations performed as a condition of the sale, and any shipping charges.

If you do not purchase or make items to sell, or purchase animals for resale, you will have no inventory, and you may want to skip the rest of this section on business inventory management.

Here are a few real-life examples of how inventory costs are calculated.

Example #1: *Gordy designed a board game. All money spent on individual pieces needed to create the game must be added together, and that total amount would be divided by the total number of games Gordy assembled from those pieces.*

Gordy spent $1500 total and made 500 games, so he simply divides the cost ($1500) by the inventory (500) to get the cost per game. The cost per game is $3 in this example.

Any time Gordy removes a game from his inventory he gets to deduct $3. If Gordy sells 300 games this tax year, and the remaining 200 the following tax year he would deduct $900 the first year and $600 the second.

All samples and any damaged inventory are considered sold when removed from inventory.

Example #2: *Cheryl publishes a cookbook she wrote. Cheryl should include all costs involved in producing the book with her first print run costs; future printings include only "update" expenses and new production and printing costs.*

Since Cheryl spent $6,000 on production and printing expenses, and she printed 3,000 books she will deduct $2 for every book sold, given away, or trashed during the tax year.

It took five years for Cheryl to sell all of the cookbooks and her inventory deductions were as follows: Year one 700 sold ($1400 expensed), year two 1,000 sold ($2,000 expensed), year three 625 sold ($1250 expensed), year four 550 sold ($1100 expensed) and year five 125 sold ($250 expensed). Expenses total the $6,000 spent; it was just posted to offset income as it came in, during the year of sale, as required by the IRS.

Example #3: *Eugene travels to Europe on vacation and paints a picture of the Eiffel Tower. After returning home he receives so many compliments on the painting that he pays to have a limited edition printed, and offers them for sale.*

Because his trip to Europe was a vacation, the travel bills are not a business expense.

However, Eugene paid $2,000 to produce 200 prints, spent $600 for 200 mats and $100 for packaging, so he has a total of $2,700 in inventory expenses. Divide that $2,700 by 200 finished prints and he has a cost of $13.50 per print.

If Eugene sells 100 prints the first year, 80 the second year, and 20 the third year, his deductions will be $1350 in year one, $1080 in year two, and $270 in year three. Total deductions are $2,700 divided over the three year time period it took for all of the prints to be sold.

Example #4: *Roger designs a tattoo poster explaining how to care for your new tattoo and sells them to his customers for $4 each. To print 200 mini posters Roger paid $210. If you divide 200 into $210 you learn that those posters cost him $1.05 each.*

In the three years it took Roger to sell all 200 posters his inventory deductions were as follows: Year one 70 posters were sold ($74 expensed), year two 117 sold ($123 expensed) and in year three the last 13 were sold and that last $13 was deducted.

Recording New Inventory

You will find two New Inventory Report forms on pages 73 and 74.

In Column (1) enter the name of the item purchased for resale and how many units.

Column (2) will include every penny you spent to purchase this item. To get this figure you will add all of your purchase or assembly costs and shipping expenses together. Enter this total in Column (2).

The number in Column (3) is obtained by dividing Column (2) - Total Cost by Column (1) - Number of Items Purchased.

In future years, enter all new items purchased for resale onto a New Inventory Report as it arrives, completing columns 1-3 at that time. You can fill out the rest of the columns on the last work day of the year, when you count the end of year inventory.

In Column (4) enter how many of this item were sold, trashed or donated; in other words every item removed from your saleable inventory during the tax year. To determine this number complete your inventory count for Column (6) and subtract the opening inventory count for the year.

Column (5) is figured by multiplying Column (3) x Column (4). That is the value assigned to all of the items sold this year.

Inventory is always counted on the last working day of the tax year. Simply count the items remaining in stock, both in your office as well as items unsold in another's inventory, and enter that number in Column (6).

Column (7) is figured by multiplying Column (3) x Column (6).

Column (5) contains the total cost of items sold, and is the amount you can deduct from this year's inventory expense.

Recording Prior Year Inventory

You will find two Prior Year Inventory Report forms on pages 75 and 76.

In Column (1) enter the item and how many units remained in inventory at the beginning of the tax year.

Column (2) is the same cost per item dollar amount you used to report inventory sold in prior years. Enter the Cost per Item in the second column.

The number in Column (3) reflects how many items you sold, trashed or were donated. You can determine this figure by counting the inventory remaining at the end of the year and subtracting that from the opening inventory for the same year.

Column (4) is determined by multiplying Column (2) x Column (3). That is the total value assigned to all sales of this particular item, and will be the amount you get to deduct on your tax return.

On the last day of the tax year, count all remaining inventory and enter that number in Column (5).

Column (6) is determined by multiplying Column (2) x Column (5). This is the total deductible value of inventory remaining unsold.

Once you have the details posted to your New and Prior Year Inventory Reports, you can write new and prior year inventory totals on the front of the Inventory envelope, and put all inventory receipts inside.

MONTHLY EXPENSE REPORTS

The reports on the following pages cover one 12-month tax year. Each month enter the total cost for all items purchased in each category onto the proper form. At the end of the year, those categories will be added and the totals posted to an annual report for the preparation of your tax return.

Because all of the necessary forms are bound together into one book, taking this entire book to the tax professional's office will put all necessary back-up information at hand. Post your expenses monthly and you'll have one more way to show the IRS just how serious you are about making money.

Go back to the front of this book and enter the tax year for the records you are currently posting. This organizer can also be a handy tool in assessing the financial position of your business.

Inventory report forms are located on pages 73-76, behind the monthly expense forms. If you do not purchase items for resale, or if you sell everything the same year it is purchased, you will not have inventory.

At the end of each tax year any business with inventory is required to count all remaining inventory, both in the office and out for sale on consignment.

JANUARY
MONTHLY EXPENSE REPORT

A	Advertising & Promotional Expenses	$
B	Banks, Visa & Other Business Interest Paid	$
C	Cleaning Materials & Business Supplies	$
D	Donations to Nonprofit Organizations	$
E	Educational Seminars & Classes	$
F	Fix-it & Repair Expenses	$
G	Gifts	$
H	Home Office Expenses	$
I	Insurance	$
J	Job Required Licenses & Dues	$
K	Key Operating Expenses	$
L	Legal & Professional Fees	$
M	Meals & Entertainment	$
N	Newspapers, Magazines & Subscriptions	$

	JANUARY MONTHLY EXPENSE REPORT – page 2	
O	Office Supplies	$
P	Percentages, Commissions & Fees Paid to Others	$
Q	Equipment Purchased	$
R	Rent Paid	$
S	Shipping & Postage	$
T	Travel	$
U	Utilities	$
V	Vehicle (Car/Truck) Expenses	$
W	Wages & Contract Labor Expenses	$
X	Taxes Paid	$
Y	Your Exhibit, Tournament or Entry Expenses	$
Z	Inventory	$

Additional Information:

	FEBRUARY MONTHLY EXPENSE REPORT	
A	Advertising & Promotional Expenses	$
B	Banks, Visa & Other Business Interest Paid	$
C	Cleaning Materials & Business Supplies	$
D	Donations to Nonprofit Organizations	$
E	Educational Seminars & Classes	$
F	Fix-it & Repair Expenses	$
G	Gifts	$
H	Home Office Expenses	$
I	Insurance	$
J	Job Required Licenses & Dues	$
K	Key Operating Expenses	$
L	Legal & Professional Fees	$
M	Meals & Entertainment	$
N	Newspapers, Magazines & Subscriptions	$

	FEBRUARY MONTHLY EXPENSE REPORT – page 2	
O	Office Supplies	$
P	Percentages, Commissions & Fees Paid to Others	$
Q	Equipment Purchased	$
R	Rent Paid	$
S	Shipping & Postage	$
T	Travel	$
U	Utilities	$
V	Vehicle (Car/Truck) Expenses	$
W	Wages & Contract Labor Expenses	$
X	Taxes Paid	$
Y	Your Exhibit, Tournament or Entry Expenses	$
Z	Inventory	$
Additional Information:		

	MARCH MONTHLY EXPENSE REPORT	
A	Advertising & Promotional Expenses	$
B	Banks, Visa & Other Business Interest Paid	$
C	Cleaning Materials & Business Supplies	$
D	Donations to Nonprofit Organizations	$
E	Educational Seminars & Classes	$
F	Fix-it & Repair Expenses	$
G	Gifts	$
H	Home Office Expenses	$
I	Insurance	$
J	Job Required Licenses & Dues	$
K	Key Operating Expenses	$
L	Legal & Professional Fees	$
M	Meals & Entertainment	$
N	Newspapers, Magazines & Subscriptions	$

	MARCH MONTHLY EXPENSE REPORT – page 2	
O	Office Supplies	$
P	Percentages, Commissions & Fees Paid to Others	$
Q	Equipment Purchased	$
R	Rent Paid	$
S	Shipping & Postage	$
T	Travel	$
U	Utilities	$
V	Vehicle (Car/Truck) Expenses	$
W	Wages & Contract Labor Expenses	$
X	Taxes Paid	$
Y	Your Exhibit, Tournament or Entry Expenses	$
Z	Inventory	$
Additional Information:		

APRIL MONTHLY EXPENSE REPORT		
A	Advertising & Promotional Expenses	$
B	Banks, Visa & Other Business Interest Paid	$
C	Cleaning Materials & Business Supplies	$
D	Donations to Nonprofit Organizations	$
E	Educational Seminars & Classes	$
F	Fix-it & Repair Expenses	$
G	Gifts	$
H	Home Office Expenses	$
I	Insurance	$
J	Job Required Licenses & Dues	$
K	Key Operating Expenses	$
L	Legal & Professional Fees	$
M	Meals & Entertainment	$
N	Newspapers, Magazines & Subscriptions	$

	APRIL MONTHLY EXPENSE REPORT – page 2	
O	Office Supplies	$
P	Percentages, Commissions & Fees Paid to Others	$
Q	Equipment Purchased	$
R	Rent Paid	$
S	Shipping & Postage	$
T	Travel	$
U	Utilities	$
V	Vehicle (Car/Truck) Expenses	$
W	Wages & Contract Labor Expenses	$
X	Taxes Paid	$
Y	Your Exhibit, Tournament or Entry Expenses	$
Z	Inventory	$
Additional Information:		

MAY MONTHLY EXPENSE REPORT		
A	Advertising & Promotional Expenses	$
B	Banks, Visa & Other Business Interest Paid	$
C	Cleaning Materials & Business Supplies	$
D	Donations to Nonprofit Organizations	$
E	Educational Seminars & Classes	$
F	Fix-it & Repair Expenses	$
G	Gifts	$
H	Home Office Expenses	$
I	Insurance	$
J	Job Required Licenses & Dues	$
K	Key Operating Expenses	$
L	Legal & Professional Fees	$
M	Meals & Entertainment	$
N	Newspapers, Magazines & Subscriptions	$

MAY MONTHLY EXPENSE REPORT – page 2		
O	Office Supplies	$
P	Percentages, Commissions & Fees Paid to Others	$
Q	Equipment Purchased	$
R	Rent Paid	$
S	Shipping & Postage	$
T	Travel	$
U	Utilities	$
V	Vehicle (Car/Truck) Expenses	$
W	Wages & Contract Labor Expenses	$
X	Taxes Paid	$
Y	Your Exhibit, Tournament or Entry Expenses	$
Z	Inventory	$
Additional Information:		

	JUNE MONTHLY EXPENSE REPORT	
A	Advertising & Promotional Expenses	$
B	Banks, Visa & Other Business Interest Paid	$
C	Cleaning Materials & Business Supplies	$
D	Donations to Nonprofit Organizations	$
E	Educational Seminars & Classes	$
F	Fix-it & Repair Expenses	$
G	Gifts	$
H	Home Office Expenses	$
I	Insurance	$
J	Job Required Licenses & Dues	$
K	Key Operating Expenses	$
L	Legal & Professional Fees	$
M	Meals & Entertainment	$
N	Newspapers, Magazines & Subscriptions	$

JUNE MONTHLY EXPENSE REPORT – page 2		
O	Office Supplies	$
P	Percentages, Commissions & Fees Paid to Others	$
Q	Equipment Purchased	$
R	Rent Paid	$
S	Shipping & Postage	$
T	Travel	$
U	Utilities	$
V	Vehicle (Car/Truck) Expenses	$
W	Wages & Contract Labor Expenses	$
X	Taxes Paid	$
Y	Your Exhibit, Tournament or Entry Expenses	$
Z	Inventory	$
Additional Information:		

	JULY MONTHLY EXPENSE REPORT	
A	Advertising & Promotional Expenses	$
B	Banks, Visa & Other Business Interest Paid	$
C	Cleaning Materials & Business Supplies	$
D	Donations to Nonprofit Organizations	$
E	Educational Seminars & Classes	$
F	Fix-it & Repair Expenses	$
G	Gifts	$
H	Home Office Expenses	$
I	Insurance	$
J	Job Required Licenses & Dues	$
K	Key Operating Expenses	$
L	Legal & Professional Fees	$
M	Meals & Entertainment	$
N	Newspapers, Magazines & Subscriptions	$

	JULY MONTHLY EXPENSE REPORT – page 2	
O	Office Supplies	$
P	Percentages, Commissions & Fees Paid to Others	$
Q	Equipment Purchased	$
R	Rent Paid	$
S	Shipping & Postage	$
T	Travel	$
U	Utilities	$
V	Vehicle (Car/Truck) Expenses	$
W	Wages & Contract Labor Expenses	$
X	Taxes Paid	$
Y	Your Exhibit, Tournament or Entry Expenses	$
Z	Inventory	$
Additional Information:		

	AUGUST MONTHLY EXPENSE REPORT	
A	Advertising & Promotional Expenses	$
B	Banks, Visa & Other Business Interest Paid	$
C	Cleaning Materials & Business Supplies	$
D	Donations to Nonprofit Organizations	$
E	Educational Seminars & Classes	$
F	Fix-it & Repair Expenses	$
G	Gifts	$
H	Home Office Expenses	$
I	Insurance	$
J	Job Required Licenses & Dues	$
K	Key Operating Expenses	$
L	Legal & Professional Fees	$
M	Meals & Entertainment	$
N	Newspapers, Magazines & Subscriptions	$

	AUGUST MONTHLY EXPENSE REPORT – page 2	
O	Office Supplies	$
P	Percentages, Commissions & Fees Paid to Others	$
Q	Equipment Purchased	$
R	Rent Paid	$
S	Shipping & Postage	$
T	Travel	$
U	Utilities	$
V	Vehicle (Car/Truck) Expenses	$
W	Wages & Contract Labor Expenses	$
X	Taxes Paid	$
Y	Your Exhibit, Tournament or Entry Expenses	$
Z	Inventory	$
Additional Information:		

	SEPTEMBER MONTHLY EXPENSE REPORT	
A	Advertising & Promotional Expenses	$
B	Banks, Visa & Other Business Interest Paid	$
C	Cleaning Materials & Business Supplies	$
D	Donations to Nonprofit Organizations	$
E	Educational Seminars & Classes	$
F	Fix-it & Repair Expenses	$
G	Gifts	$
H	Home Office Expenses	$
I	Insurance	$
J	Job Required Licenses & Dues	$
K	Key Operating Expenses	$
L	Legal & Professional Fees	$
M	Meals & Entertainment	$
N	Newspapers, Magazines & Subscriptions	$

	SEPTEMBER MONTHLY EXPENSE REPORT – page 2	
O	Office Supplies	$
P	Percentages, Commissions & Fees Paid to Others	$
Q	Equipment Purchased	$
R	Rent Paid	$
S	Shipping & Postage	$
T	Travel	$
U	Utilities	$
V	Vehicle (Car/Truck) Expenses	$
W	Wages & Contract Labor Expenses	$
X	Taxes Paid	$
Y	Your Exhibit, Tournament or Entry Expenses	$
Z	Inventory	$
Additional Information:		

	OCTOBER MONTHLY EXPENSE REPORT	
A	Advertising & Promotional Expenses	$
B	Banks, Visa & Other Business Interest Paid	$
C	Cleaning Materials & Business Supplies	$
D	Donations to Nonprofit Organizations	$
E	Educational Seminars & Classes	$
F	Fix-it & Repair Expenses	$
G	Gifts	$
H	Home Office Expenses	$
I	Insurance	$
J	Job Required Licenses & Dues	$
K	Key Operating Expenses	$
L	Legal & Professional Fees	$
M	Meals & Entertainment	$
N	Newspapers, Magazines & Subscriptions	$

	OCTOBER MONTHLY EXPENSE REPORT – page 2	
O	Office Supplies	$
P	Percentages, Commissions & Fees Paid to Others	$
Q	Equipment Purchased	$
R	Rent Paid	$
S	Shipping & Postage	$
T	Travel	$
U	Utilities	$
V	Vehicle (Car/Truck) Expenses	$
W	Wages & Contract Labor Expenses	$
X	Taxes Paid	$
Y	Your Exhibit, Tournament or Entry Expenses	$
Z	Inventory	$
Additional Information:		

	NOVEMBER MONTHLY EXPENSE REPORT	
A	Advertising & Promotional Expenses	$
B	Banks, Visa & Other Business Interest Paid	$
C	Cleaning Materials & Business Supplies	$
D	Donations to Nonprofit Organizations	$
E	Educational Seminars & Classes	$
F	Fix-it & Repair Expenses	$
G	Gifts	$
H	Home Office Expenses	$
I	Insurance	$
J	Job Required Licenses & Dues	$
K	Key Operating Expenses	$
L	Legal & Professional Fees	$
M	Meals & Entertainment	$
N	Newspapers, Magazines & Subscriptions	$

	NOVEMBER MONTHLY EXPENSE REPORT – page 2	
O	Office Supplies	$
P	Percentages, Commissions & Fees Paid to Others	$
Q	Equipment Purchased	$
R	Rent Paid	$
S	Shipping & Postage	$
T	Travel	$
U	Utilities	$
V	Vehicle (Car/Truck) Expenses	$
W	Wages & Contract Labor Expenses	$
X	Taxes Paid	$
Y	Your Exhibit, Tournament or Entry Expenses	$
Z	Inventory	$
Additional Information:		

DECEMBER MONTHLY EXPENSE REPORT		
A	Advertising & Promotional Expenses	$
B	Banks, Visa & Other Business Interest Paid	$
C	Cleaning Materials & Business Supplies	$
D	Donations to Nonprofit Organizations	$
E	Educational Seminars & Classes	$
F	Fix-it & Repair Expenses	$
G	Gifts	$
H	Home Office Expenses	$
I	Insurance	$
J	Job Required Licenses & Dues	$
K	Key Operating Expenses	$
L	Legal & Professional Fees	$
M	Meals & Entertainment	$
N	Newspapers, Magazines & Subscriptions	$

DECEMBER MONTHLY EXPENSE REPORT – page 2		
O	Office Supplies	$
P	Percentages, Commissions & Fees Paid to Others	$
Q	Equipment Purchased	$
R	Rent Paid	$
S	Shipping & Postage	$
T	Travel	$
U	Utilities	$
V	Vehicle (Car/Truck) Expenses	$
W	Wages & Contract Labor Expenses	$
X	Taxes Paid	$
Y	Your Exhibit, Tournament or Entry Expenses	$
Z	Inventory	$
Additional Information:		

NEW INVENTORY REPORT
(All new items added to inventory during tax year)

(1)	(2)	(3)	(4)	(5)	(6)	(7)
Product & Total Number of Items Added to Inventory	Total Cost to Add Inventory	Cost per Item. Divide Column (2) by number in Column (1)	No. Sold, Donated or Removed this year	Value of All Inventory Removed. Column (3) x Column (4)	Inventory Count at the End of the Tax Year	Inv. Value at End of Year. Column (3) x Column (6)

NEW INVENTORY REPORT – page 2
(All new items added to inventory during tax year)

(1)	(2)	(3)	(4)	(5)	(6)	(7)
Product & Total Number of Items Added to Inventory	Total Cost to Add Inventory	Cost per Item. Divide Column (2) by number in Column (1)	No. Sold, Donated or Removed this year	Value of All Inventory Removed. Column (3) x Column (4)	Inventory Count at the End of the Tax Year	Inv. Value at End of Year. Column (3) x Column (6)

PRIOR YEAR INVENTORY REPORT
(All new items added to inventory during tax year)

(1)	(2)	(3)	(4)	(5)	(6)
Product/Number Remaining in Inventory at Beginning of Year	Cost Per Item	No. Sold, Donated or Removed from Inventory	Value of Inventory Removed Column (2) x Column (3)	Inventory Count at the End of Tax Year	Value of Inventory At the End of Year Column (2) x Column (5)

PRIOR YEAR INVENTORY REPORT – page 2
(All new items added to inventory during tax year)

(1) Product/Number Remaining in Inventory at Beginning of Year	(2) Cost Per Item	(3) No. Sold, Donated or Removed from Inventory	(4) Value of Inventory Removed Column (2) x Column (3)	(5) Inventory Count at the End of Tax Year	(6) Value of Inventory At the End of Year Column (2) x Column (5)

STEP THREE: PUTTING IT ALL TOGETHER

This final step has you posting all of the expense totals you've written on the front of the Monthly Expense Reports, and other figures you've already transferred to the various forms in the next chapter. You will fill this section out for your tax professional.

When you're done, those reports will contain all of the information you or a tax professional will need to prepare your small business Schedule C tax return, or post hobby income and expenses to your personal tax return.

What to take to the Tax Professional

A tax professional can only work from the information you provide, and the more you know about business taxes the less likely it will be for you to miss valuable tax deductions.

Tax Pro Rule #8

No matter how good your tax professional is,

if you don't provide

all of the necessary information and figures,

your tax return will be wrong.

Most people leave the tax professional's office each year knowing nothing more about tax law than they did the year before. When you visit the tax pro, bring a list of questions; if he or she refuses to answer those questions go elsewhere.

When you visit your tax professional you will need to take along all of your personal income tax information, because your business profit or loss is simply posted to your personal 1040 tax return before it is filed. The tax professional will complete all supporting tax forms.

Have your taxes prepared as early in the year as possible. When you owe taxes, the money is not due until April 15th, even if you mail your tax return on January 2nd.

And remember, not all taxes are bad. Self-employment taxes fund your Social Security and Medicare, and if you don't pay much in, you won't draw much out during your senior years.

Deducting that Home Office

If you have a home office, you'll need to take the following figures to your tax preparer as well:

- Total square footage of your home. This figure can be found in your home purchase or rental documents.

- Total square footage of the area used exclusively for business. To get this figure multiply the room length by the room width; if more than one room is used you will need to add those sums together.

- Total annual amount paid for household insurance rent, repairs and lawn maintenance, utilities (electricity, water, sewer, gas, and garbage) and other household expenses that your home and business shared. If you had any expenses that were 100% home office related list those separately. You will also need your mortgage interest 1099's and tax statements if you own your home.

You will find a place to enter this information on the following page. If you choose to depreciate your home office, and it is located within your personal residence, you should discuss this with your tax professional first.

Depreciating a home office could be a 30+ year tax project, and when the house is eventually sold you will have to exclude that portion of gain from the personal residence tax shelter. Unless you know the tax laws on depreciation, this is not a decision to make alone.

If you remodel your office or home, re-roof the structure, create a separate office entrance, or make any other changes that also affect the business portion of your home, you can depreciate the business portion of those expenses as well. If you have any of these expenses, be sure to include that information here as well, and discuss them with your tax professional.

Home Office – If you have a home office your tax preparer will need the following information:

- Total square footage of your home _____.

- Total square footage used exclusively for your business _____.

- Total annual amount paid for shared utilities and other household expenses that were also used by your home office (rent, insurance, etc.), along with a breakdown of those shared expenses: $_____.

- Breakdown of any home office expenses that are 100% business expense:

Creating an Annual Tax Report

The Annual Tax Report is where you combine your monthly totals to produce one end-of-year report. You've already done most of the work necessary.

This report is broken into three sections, Business Income, Business Expenses and Inventory Figures. In brief, you will

1. Add up your monthly income to get the annual income total,

2. Add up your monthly expense report categories for annual expense totals, and

3. Complete the end of year columns on your inventory reports.

Business Income

You already have complete records of all income earned in your business in three places. The first is on your monthly bank statements, the second documentation came when you entered that monthly income onto the front of your Business Income Envelope, and the third is on your Income Tracking Sheet.

If you have not already done so, put your monthly bank statements away in the Business Income Envelope.

Go to your Income Tracking Sheet, on page 23, and total each of the three income categories. Transfer those three totals onto page 85. The sum of all three is your annual business income.

Business Expenses

Because you entered your expenses monthly, on the Monthly Expense Reports, you will find all of the information you need on those twelve two-page reports. Monthly Expense Reports begin on page 48.

Total the monthly amounts listed for each expense category and put that 12-month total on the Annual Tax Report found on pages 86-87.

If you hire employees, have vehicle expenses or business mileage, or make any tax payments during the year you will also need to fill in some additional information on the following pages. Some of this will get you better tax breaks; other information will help you to survive a tax audit. Skip any items that do not apply to your business.

Payroll Expenses – If you hire employees you will need to bring your records for payroll expenses. These would include copies of your employees' W-2's as well as figures for total wages paid, social security taxes withheld as well as paid, federal and state income taxes withheld and paid for employees, plus any other money paid out for workman's comp, local taxes or unemployment insurance.

Vehicle & Mileage – Your preparer will need mileage and vehicle information on any vehicles used in your business. Whether you have one vehicle that you use exclusively for your business, or you use your family car for business errands, you still need to keep written records. Start by listing each vehicle below:

Vehicle #1

Make & year:

Year first used in business:

Total miles driven this year in this car:

Business miles driven this year in this car:

Vehicle #2

Make & year:

Year first used in business:

Total miles driven this year in this car:

Business miles driven this year in this car:

If you have a vehicle reserved 100% for business use, it is sometimes a better value to deduct actual expenses and depreciation on the business vehicle.

If your vehicle is only for business use, list all out-of-pocket expenses paid or charged during the tax year on the following page.

Vehicle #1

Total gasoline purchased:

Total repairs, and/or parts purchased:

Total car payments made (include price if you purchased a new vehicle this year), plus car insurance and all other expenses incurred for this vehicle. Itemize those items below:

Vehicle #2

Total gasoline purchased:

Total repairs, and/or parts purchased:

Total car payments made (include price if you purchased a new vehicle this year), plus car insurance and all other expenses incurred for this vehicle. Itemize those items below:

Taxes – If you made quarterly tax payments you will need to list the total of all taxes paid below so that you can get credit on this year's tax bill. You may be making payments both to the IRS and one or more states.

Also list any sales taxes, city taxes or other local taxes paid. Be sure to include the date each payment was made.

If you received W2-G tax forms take those with you to the tax preparer's office; let the preparer know that you have included these numbers with income and listed the total of all taxes deducted below.

- Federal Quarterly Tax Payments:

- State Quarterly Tax Payments:

- Other Business Taxes Paid:

- State & Federal Taxes Withheld on 1099's received:

Inventory – If you do not buy, make or purchase items for resale, you can skip this section. If you had inventory you will need to count your remaining inventory at the end of the tax year and enter your Opening Inventory, New Inventory Added, and Closing Inventory on the following page.

Begin by counting all remaining inventory and completing your New and Prior Year Inventory Reports on pages 73-76. Once these reports are complete, you can fill in the final inventory figures below.

Opening Inventory

If you had no inventory last year, your opening inventory will be zero; otherwise it will be the same dollar figure that you showed last year as your Closing Inventory.

Opening Inventory Value for current tax year: $_____.

New Inventory Added

To get the value of all new Inventory added simply total everything in column 2 on the New Inventory Report forms. This is the total amount you spent to acquire your new inventory during the tax year.

New Inventory Value added during current tax year: $_____.

Closing Inventory

Your Closing Inventory for this tax year is calculated by adding everything in the last column on all copies of both the New and Prior Year Inventory Reports. Fill in the total figure below:

Closing Inventory Value for current tax year: $_____.

YOUR ANNUAL TAX REPORT

Nobody in a business that the IRS classifies as a hobby activity should attempt to prepare their own business taxes. You will need someone with accounting knowledge to guide your activities. Find a preparer who is already doing tax returns for others in your line of work.

A small business owner is allowed to set up a business retirement account, letting them divert a percentage of their profits for their own retirement, paying the taxes later when they expect lower earnings. A tax accountant can explain which account you qualify for and how much you can add each year.

The next chapter, **Developing an Audit-Proof Mindset**, explains what to do with all of the tax receipts and records you've organized, and how to think in a manner that will help you to avoid attracting an audit.

If you have not already done so, transfer the total of all monthly expense categories, for the entire tax year, onto the two-page report that follows. If you need additional information, it will be found on the outside of your expense envelopes.

Write your total income below. You will find those totals on page 23.

Total Bank Deposits for the Year $_____

Total Unique Income for the Year $_____

Total Barter & Other Income for the Year $_____

TOTAL BUSINESS INCOME $_____

ANNUAL TAX REPORT Tax Year _____		
A	Advertising & Promotional Expenses	$
B	Banks, Visa & Other Business Interest Paid	$
C	Cleaning Materials & Business Supplies	$
D	Donations to Nonprofit Organizations	$
E	Educational Seminars & Classes	$
F	Fix-it & Repair Expenses	$
G	Gifts	$
H	Home Office Expenses	$
I	Insurance	$
J	Job Required Licenses & Dues	$
K	Key Operating Expenses	$
L	Legal & Professional Fees	$
M	Meals & Entertainment	$
N	Newspapers, Magazines & Subscriptions	$

ANNUAL TAX REPORT – page 2
Tax Year _____

O	Office Supplies	$
P	Percentages, Commissions & Fees Paid to Others	$
Q	Equipment Purchased	$
R	Rent Paid	$
S	Shipping & Postage	$
T	Travel	$
U	Utilities	$
V	Vehicle (Car/Truck) Expenses	$
W	Wages & Contract Labor Expenses	$
X	Taxes Paid	$
Y	Your Exhibit, Tournament or Entry Expenses	$
Z	Inventory	$

Additional Information:

DEVELOPING AN AUDIT-PROOF MINDSET

Establishing an audit-proof mindset is simple. When all income and expenses for a business are kept separate from personal funds, and every income and expense has a paper trail, you almost always survive an audit.

The exception comes when you have misinterpreted tax law.

Tax Pro Rule #9

Tax laws change every year,

sometimes offering huge tax savings for only a short time.

Even if you do your own taxes,

you should go see a tax professional every 2-3 years,

especially if your business activity is classified as a hobby by the IRS.

Any time you are engaged in a business that is normally considered to be a hobby by the IRS, you should work with a qualified tax accountant to be sure your tax return is right. Hobby industries are more likely to be audited, making individual guidance by a tax accountant a necessary step in avoiding and beating an audit.

Tax Pro Rule #10

Without receipts, you will fail an audit.

Box or bag your tax receipts, and keep those records

for at least 6 years. Copies of tax returns

should be kept a minimum of 10 years.

Storage of tax records doesn't have to be fancy. Simply use a 1-2 gallon plastic food storage bag. Put the entire year's worth of receipt envelopes inside, write the tax year on the bag in indelible ink, and place that bag into a cardboard file box. If you have lots of receipts, you can store each year in a shoebox labeled with the proper tax year.

Mark your storage box "Tax Receipts"; this box needs to be large enough to hold 6-10 giant Ziploc bags, or shoeboxes, each filled with a year's worth of receipts. When the storage box is full, file it away and start another. Or, if those records are older than 6 years, remove and shred the oldest to make room for the current year.

Don't put your copy of the final tax return or your W-2's into this box. You will need a copy of that tax return and its accompanying W-2's if you apply for a mortgage or loan during the year, so store then in a more convenient place. Keeping them easily accessible will make filling out those applications easier, and you'll have all of the tax papers the bank requires handy.

This financial organizer will be useful too, so don't hide it away in the box. The numbers in this book can be helpful when writing a business plan, adjusting finances, or making inventory projections. Store it with your other business financial information.

An IRS audit may sound scary, but an audit is nothing more than a meeting where the taxpayer is expected to show the receipts that back up the numbers he or she put onto a that year's tax return. The person who has receipts is done quickly.

But, because individuals are extremely likely to say too much during an audit, exposing other issues and causing the IRS to ask for more meetings and more receipts, it's smart for any business owner to hire a tax accountant or a tax company that specializes in audits to attend that meeting for them.

If you have a regular tax professional call them the day you receive your audit letter; dealing with audits on the returns that they prepare is part of a tax professional's service. And, they can also represent you for audits on tax returns that you prepared yourself.

Take the bag containing your income and expense envelopes for the year being audited with you, as well as your "In Case of Audit" folder and this book, when you meet with the tax professional. That person will know exactly which papers will be necessary to win the audit. And, if you've followed all of the Tax Pro Rules, those receipts will be in that bag, and easy to find.

Planning for the Future

If you have inventory on your shelves at the close of the tax year, you are going to need a Prior Year Inventory Report to track remaining inventory for next year's tax records. If you will be adding new inventory you'll also need a New Inventory Report.

Get your next copy of **Do My Business Taxes Please** now, write the current year in the front, and start those two inventory reports now. Keep that new organizer where you normally receive and/or record new inventory, and use it to record new inventory as it arrives.

You'll also be ready to record expenses monthly as soon as January is over. Starting your organizer now will give you a good jump on organizing next year's tax mess, and put you on track for regular monthly accounting.

DOCUMENTING YOUR BUSINESS ACTIVITIES

If you are building your business by working part time, or involved in one of the industries classified by the IRS as a hobby activity, documenting your work activities in a business-like manner is an important part of proving to the IRS that you are business-minded.

Documenting your business activities simply means keeping track of dates and total hours during which you perform business activities and make sales efforts. Working on a regular schedule and tracking sales efforts to see which ones pay off are two important keys to performing in a profit-minded manner. Business owners who fail to analyze their marketing efforts may be spending money unwisely.

The following pages contain forms for documenting part-time business activities, or you can create your own log in a spiral notebook. A notebook actually works better for some occupations because you can design your own headings and allow space for detailing the work accomplished or completion of goals.

If you are audited, be sure to let your tax professional know that you have these records as well.

THE SOLE-PROPRIETOR'S LOG BOOK				
Date	Project or Marketing Activity	Total Work Time	Results of Activity	Is Follow-up Necessary?

THE SOLE-PROPRIETOR'S LOG BOOK - page 2				
Date	Project or Marketing Activity	Total Work Time	Results of Activity	Is Follow-up Necessary?

THE SOLE-PROPRIETOR'S LOG BOOK - page 3				
Date	Project or Marketing Activity	Total Work Time	Results of Activity	Is Follow-up Necessary?

THE SOLE-PROPRIETOR'S LOG BOOK - page 4

Date	Project or Marketing Activity	Total Work Time	Results of Activity	Is Follow-up Necessary?

	THE SOLE-PROPRIETOR'S LOG BOOK - page 5			
Date	Project or Marketing Activity	Total Work Time	Results of Activity	Is Follow-up Necessary?

INDEX

THREE NEW TITLES BY KIKI CANNIFF

CREATIVITY IS MY BUSINESS - A Financial Organizer for Freelance Artists, Musicians, Photographers, Writers & Other Talented Individuals

The IRS classifies creative activities as a hobby, claiming that those who are creative do it for fun, not as a business. And, when a person participates in creative activities part-time this is a hard label to dodge, unless you keep proper records. This financial organizer shows creative individuals how to track their sales and creative efforts in a manner that will show the IRS they are running a business. It includes all forms necessary for regular recordkeeping as well as for preparing income and expense figures for annual tax preparation. This system does not require a computer or any bookkeeping knowledge.

GAMBLING IS MY BUSINESS

A Financial Organizer for Professional Card Players & Other Gamblers

Learn what it takes to qualify as a professional gambler in the eyes of the IRS, and how to beat an audit of your gambling activities. This book explains the difference between gambling as a hobby vs. gambling as a business at tax time, and teaches gamblers how to track their income, expenses and gambling activities in a manner that will let them take every deduction deserved. It includes everything you need for regular recordkeeping as well as for preparing income and expense figures for your tax preparer. This system is simple and does not require a computer or any bookkeeping knowledge.

DO MY PERSONAL TAXES PLEASE - A Financial Organizer for U.S. Taxpayers & Their Tax Professionals

If you're looking for a way to get that personal tax mess organized and pay less income tax, this book will make it easy. It explains IRS tax rules as they apply to individuals and families in easy-to-understand terms, and will show you how to make our tax laws work for you, what you need to take with you when you visit your tax professional, what to do if you withdraw retirement funds or suffer a loss, how to qualify for bigger tax refunds, what to do when a family member dies or retires, and how to use tax credits to secure your future. This system requires no computer or bookkeeping knowledge; you simply record each event in the organizer when it happens, and take the organizer to your tax preparer.

For more information on books by KiKi Canniff visit www.OneMorePress.com